MW01257723

North Indian Cookbook

Hemant Kumar

Copyright © 2015 Royal Book Publishers. All rights reserved. No part of this book shall be reproduced, stored in a retrieval system, or transmitted by any means—electronic, mechanical, photocopying, recording, or otherwise—without written permission from the publisher, except for the inclusion of brief quotations in a review.

Every effort has been made to make this book as complete and as accurate as possible, but no warranty of completeness is implied. The information is provided on an as-is basis. The authors and the publisher shall have neither liability nor responsibility to any person or entity with respect to any loss or damages arising from the information contained in this book.

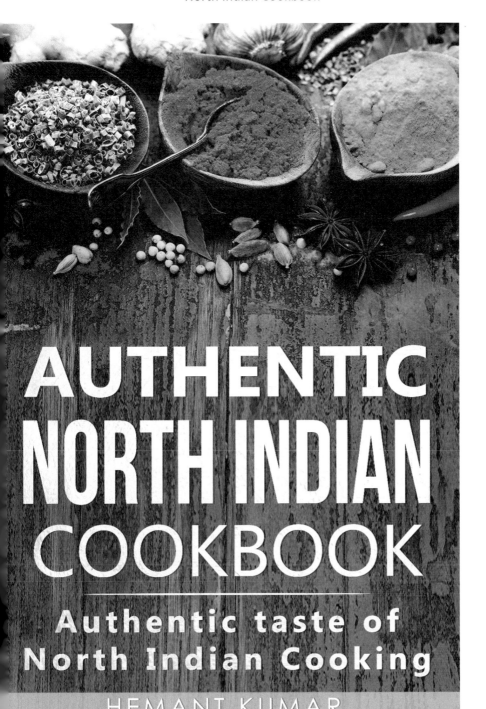

AUTHENTIC NORTH INDIAN COOKBOOK

Authentic taste of North Indian Cooking

HEMANT KUMAR

Table of Contents

Introduction 7

Utensils for North Indian Cuisine 9

Common Spices Used in Indian Cuisine 11

Entree's 17

Chicken Karahi 17

Egg Curry 19

Chicken Korma 22

Keema mutter 25

Spicy Fish Curry 28

Masala Zinga 30

Goan Prawns Curry 32

Achari Chicken 35

Saag Chicken 37

Chicken Jalfrezi..39

Appetizers 41

Chapli Kabab 41

Mutton Chops in a curry 44

Tandoori Chicken 47

Seekh Kabob 50

Vegetarian Dishes 53

Aloo Mutter Sabzi 53

Green Bean Sabzi 56

Baigan Bharta 58

Cholay Masala 60

Dal Tadka 63

Masoor ki Daal 65

Rice Dishes 67

Khichri 67

Jeera Rice 70

Hyderabadi Chicken Dum Biryani..............................73

Mutton Biryani 76

Basmati Pulao 79

Breads 81

Roti Paratha 81

Keema Paratha...84

Aloo Paratha 86

Poori...89

Soups 91

Chicken Soup 91

Tomato Soup 93

Chutneys 95

Poodina Chutney 95

Raita 97

Green Coriander Chutney 99

Deserts 100

Mango Lassi 100

Masala Chai 102

Gajar ka Halwa 104

Gulab Jamun 106

Final word 109

Introduction

India is a land of diverse culture. From dialect to cuisine, you will find wide range of diversity throughout the country. Speaking of Indian cuisine, it is famous all over the world. India has some of the most delicious and mouthwatering dishes to offer. India is known as the "land of spices"; no wonder Indian cuisine is something special. Indian food was localized up until the British rule. After India was colonized by the British, they started taking Indian recipes out of India and this is how Indian food gained fame all over the world.

You will find different flavor of food in different parts of India. Are you looking for something spicy and colorful? Then North Indian cuisine would just be the perfect option for you. It is a nice blend of different types of spices which gives North Indian cuisine its unique flavor altogether. From Biryani to Chole, every single item is marked with its own special flavor and taste.

North Indian food is popular all over the country. There are more than 200 different dishes in the North Indian dishes. Besides, you will find a wide variety of rice items along with different side dishes that include vegetables, fish, goat mutton etc.

The influence of Mughal cuisine is quite prominent in North Indian food. Mughals ruled over India for more than 700 years and it's no wonder that some of their traditions and legacies are still being followed. Talking of Mughlai cuisine, the list is endless; however, the one which is most popular, not only in India but in other South-Asian Countries is Biryani. If you wish to experience the true blend of all kinds of spices along with meat or chicken, then this is one dish which you cannot afford to miss!

Specifically for North Indian cuisine the state of Punjab has a huge influence. There are wide range of Punjabi dishes which are popular all over the country. From chicken tandoori to makki di roti; Punjab has wide varieties dishes to offer. Its all about taste and aroma. From Kabab to Biryani; every single item has its own special and unique flavor to it.

Utensils for North Indian Cuisine

In North Indian cooking there are wide ranges of utensils that are being used. Here is info on some of them:

Karai or kadai : Also known as the wok, a karai is perhaps the most common utensil found in Indian kitchens. It is used for cooking all kinds of foods and usually is made of copper bottoms. There are karai with stainless steel bottom also available; however, they are not very effective as there is possibility of food getting burned quite easily. A karai is usually used for deep-frying, sautéing and regular frying. It is one of the most versatile utensil found in an Indian kitchen

Pressure Cooker: Meat and lentils are some of the most common Indian foods that are cooked daily. In order to make sure that they are cooked well they are cooked at high heat for some time. A regular pot might not prove to be quite effective as there are certain items that are required to be cooked for a long period of time. This is where pressure cookers come into the picture. They are very effective when it comes to cooking goat meat or daal. As the name suggests, they subject the food to high pressure which allows the food to be cooked faster and also makes it tender. Besides, pressure cookers are also more environmentally friendly as there is a very little amount of heat wastage.

Tawa: A tawa is a traditional Indian skillet. This is commonly used for roasting which comes very handy while preparing roti or parathas. Besides, a tawa can also be used for the purpose of frying bread and also to make crepes. A tawa is usually made of cast iron. These days, non-stick tawas are available in the market.

Chakla & Belan: It is nothing but a pair of utensils that consist of a round platform which is used to roll and mold the dough and a rolling pin. This is a common utensil found in Indian kitchens and is essential when it comes to cooking naan and chapati.

Spice Grinders: North Indian cuisine is known to be spicy. A spice grinder is a device which is used to grind whole spices. With a spice grinder, there is no need to buy ready-made spice powders from the market, which contain artificial additive flavor and color.

Handi: It is a type of deep pot which comes with a wide rim. Usually, a handi is used for the purpose of cooking rice and Biryani, pulao, etc.

Degchi: This is another very common utensil to be used in Indian kitchens. A degchi is quite similar to that of a handi and is used for slow cooking of food. One of the most important features of a degchi is it comes with a heavy bottom which lets the heat get transferred to the food properly and in a controlled manner. This makes sure that the foods don't get burned and maintains uniformity. Apart from using it for slow cooking, a degchi is also used for boiling milk

Colanders: There are many vegetables used in North Indian dishes. It is important to have a colander as it is used for cleaning and draining the vegetables before they are being cooked.

These are some of the most common types of utensils that are used for preparing North Indian cuisines. Apart from these, there are other kinds of utensils also in use but not covered here.

Common Spices Used in Indian Cuisine

What makes North Indian cuisine so special is the fact that you will find a blend of different spices. For more than thousands of years India has been the largest producers of spices; as a matter of fact, the use of spices in food were first introduced in India. So, no wonder Indian food would be full of spices. There is a wide number of types of spices used in Indian cuisines.

Here are some of the most commonly used ones:

Cardamom: In India, there are two types of cardamoms that are used, they are Green and Black.

Green Cardamom: It is the most commonly used variety of cardamom in India and is used in almost all kinds of dishes from Biryani to Lassi. The flavor of green cardamom is sweet and light with a mild touch of eucalyptus. Green cardamom plays an important role while preparing spice mixes; Garam Masala for example.

Black Cardamom: Black cardamom is smoky and very powerful and needs to be used very carefully and with caution. Usually, only the seeds of the black cardamom are used

Clove: Clove is another common spice used in North Indian cuisine and offers a unique flavor to the dishes. It has a very strong flavor. Technically, cloves are flowers and the oils are extracted before they are dried out and used for cooking. Cloves can be blended into spice mixes or can be used separately. While using cloves it is important to be careful as it has the capability to overpower other delicate spices.

Cassia Bark: Cassia bark is also known by the name of Chinese cinnamon and is a very interesting spice. Cassia is relatively cheaper than cinnamon and as a result, it has turned out to be one of the most popular spices to be used in Indian cuisines. It comes with a mild flavor and can be used in large proportions. Cassia can also be used in spice mix . It can be easily recognized by its rough texture. While fresh, they would smell like cinnamon. It is a perfect substitute for Cinnamon.

Black Pepper: Black peppers are grown at the Malabar region and the Western Ghats and is native to India. Growing black pepper can be a difficult process as there are different natural cycles it needs to go through. In order to grow black pepper, there has to be a particular amount of rainfall. The fact that they depend mostly on nature, the prices of black pepper varies a lot. Prior to blending, it is very important to toast the black pepper. This would give the best flavors.

Cumin: Cumin is one of the most common ingredient in spice mixes and they add a smoky note to the dishes. It is quite easy to identify cumin as they have a rough brown seed and comes with an intense fragrance. At times it can be confused with caraway, anise seeds, and fennel; however, it can be differentiated by its color. Cumin is primarily used for its intense flavor.

Coriander: Coriander is yet another common spice that is used not only in North Indian cuisines but throughout India. It is said to be one of the oldest known spices and is characterized by its golden color and ridged texture. Coriander seeds are very aromatic.

Nutmeg and Mace: Nutmeg and Mace are frequently used in all kinds of Indian dishes. Both these spices are known for their aroma and at the same time, they add a warm flavor to the dish. However, using too much of these two spices can add a touch of bitterness to the dish

Mustard Seeds: When it comes to mustard seeds, they can be black, yellow or even brown in color and are used commonly in Indian cooking. The true flavor of the mustard seeds can be felt when they are cooked in oil or are crushed. They come with a nutty and smoky flavor and mustard oil is used for the purpose of frying different items.

Fenugreek: This is a spice used all over the country. It comes with a yellowish texture. They are commonly used in the spicy dishes like butter chicken, mutton masala and others. They have a strong fragrance, and just like cloves, they need to be used very carefully.

Turmeric: Most of the Indian cuisine would remain incomplete without the use of turmeric. It can be used in a dried form or fresh. Turmeric comes with tons of different types of health benefits and is very useful to treat cuts and infections. This is a spice used in curries.

Saffron: Saffron is considered to be one of the most expensive spices in the world. Lot of hard work goes in the process of producing and making saffron. These are the stigma of crocus flowers and needs to be handpicked. The best saffron in India is produced in Kashmir and it comes with a unique flavor and has an excellent fragrance. Saffron is an intense spice and is used in special dishes like Biryani

Hing: Another very common spice to be used in North Indian cuisines. Hing is known for its smell.

Mustard Seeds and oil: Mustard oil is used in all kinds of North Indian cuisines. This oil is rich and comes with a strong smell. The oil is extracted from the mustard seeds.

These are some of the common spices used in North Indian cuisine. Apart from these, there are other spices that are also used. For preparing an Indian dish, these spices are absolutely indispensable. As a matter of fact, most of the North Indian dishes owe a lot these spices for their taste and flavor. Indian cuisines without these spices would be dull and tasteless. Therefore, it is very important to understand as to how much spices should be used. It is also important to remember that overusing these spices can ruin the dish.

These above spices can be used to make some spice mixes like garam masala, lets cover that next.

Garam Masala: When it comes to Indian cuisine, Garam Masala is one of the most common ingredients to be used. It is nothing but a blend of different types of spices. Here are some of the different types of spices that are used in preparing Garam Masala:

- Cumin
- Coriander
- Cloves
- Cardamom
- Cinnamon
- Black Pepper
- Nutmeg

There are other variations of Garam Masala that are used which includes other ingredients in addition to these like saffron, turmeric, ginger, fennel seeds, mace, mustard seeds, tamarind, star anise, bay leaves, and fenugreek.

North Indian cuisine is all about its rich taste and mouth watering flavor. Garam Masala has a major role to play in giving it this flavor.

Garlic: The use of garlic in Indian cuisines goes back to thousands of years. If you are looking for a spicy and rich dish, then it would be incomplete without the use of garlic. Garlic gives a raw smell and also helps to balance the flavor. Not to mention that garlic comes with tons of different types of health benefits

Ginger: Ginger is yet another common root used in Indian cuisine. It can be used in the form of powder and use of ginger juice is also very common. Ginger is known for its ability to fight against different types of ailments like flu, common cold, nausea and others

Mint: Though not used as frequently as finger, garlic and some other spices; mint has its own significance. It helps to add that extra flavor to the food

Onions: When it comes to North Indian cuisines, they remain incomplete without the use of onions. Onions has a lot to do with the richness and strong flavor that North Indian cuisines carry. Besides, onion also has a wide range of different types of health benefits. It helps in the process of digestion and also contains useful antioxidants.

Now that we have covered all the spices, Lets dive into the recipes . You will find recipes divided into sections like Entree's, vegetarian entree's, rice items, breads and deserts.

Entree's

Chicken Karahi

Chicken Karahi is one of the most popular North Indian dishes, if you are looking for spicy succulent chicken curry to eat with a naan. This is one of the most often used curries in Northern India region.

When it comes to preparing this dish, it's quite simple.

Ingredients:

- 300 to 400 gm boneless chicken (can substitute for boned chicken)
- Green Peeper chopped 1 cup
- Onion ½ cup

- Chopped tomatoes ¾ cup
- 2 tbsp cooking oil
- 1-2 piece broken red chili
- Cumin seeds ½ tsp
- Garlic paste
- Salt
- Chili powder
- Cashew nuts
- Finely chopped Coriander leaves

Preparation:

- Take cooking oil in a kadai (deep cooking pot) and start the heat
- Fry onions and capsicum in this oil and then keep them aside in a plate
- Add cumin and chili to the same kadai and fry them well
- Add sliced onion to it and fry till it turns into golden color
- Now add chicken pieces to it and fry for 4-5 minutes
- Add chili powder and garlic paste and keep cooking for few more minutes
- Add tomato paste and cover the pot. Cook 30 minutes or till chicken becomes soft and tender
- Then add fried onions and capsicum as garnish and then cook for another 10 minutes to let the flavors soak in.

Your delicious Chicken Karahi is ready to be served with naan or rice. Besides, it can also be used as a side dish with Biryani dishes.

Egg Curry

Egg curry is one of the most common dishes throughout India and can be used for dinner with roti, rice, paratha and puri. If cooked with good spices, it can really be very delicious. Here is a recipe to prepare egg curry.

Ingredients:

- 6 Peeled and boiled eggs
- 1 hopped onions
- Sliced ginger (small piece)
- Red chili powder ¾ teaspoon
- Tamarind paste 1 teaspoon
- Refined oil
- few Black mustard seeds
- Chopped tomatoes -2 small to medium
- few Curry leaves
- Salt
- Coconut milk to thicken the gravy

Preparation:

- Add oil in a pan and start heat on medium flame and then add mustard seeds and fry for 30 seconds. Then add chopped onions and fry them till they turn light brown in color. Then the chopped green chilies and the cinnamon need to be added. The entire mixture needs to be fried for a couple of minutes

- Add turmeric powder, ginger, the red chili powder and stir fry for a minute. These spices should be cooked till the oil starts to spate

- Then fry the boiled eggs in a separate pan over small quantity of oil. And add them to the mixture that was prepared in the first step. Then add the remaining spices to it and finally, add little coconut milk. It should be cooked in low fame and would require at least 20 minutes to get ready. After 20 minutes take it down from the heat.

Hot and delicious egg curry is now ready to be served.

Chicken Korma

Chicken korma another popular North Indian dishes and has now become popular all over the world. This mouth watering dish was first introduced by the Mughals some 500 years ago and still remains popular. Here is the recipe to prepare this delicious dish

Ingredients:

- 1 lb chicken
- Oil ½ cup
- 2-3 tsp ghee
- 6-7 Cloves
- 5-6 Cardamoms
- 1 tbsp coriander powder
- 2 tbsp garlic paste
- salt
- 1 tsp chili powder
- 1 cup yogurt
- 1 tsp ginger paste
- 1 tsp garam masala
- 2 onions sliced
- Coriander Leaves
- Saffron

Preparation:

- At first the spices need to be dry roasted in a pan and then add some ghee into them
- Add cardamom, garlic, cloves and then mix them properly
- Add the chicken pieces and cook it for 3 minutes, keep stirring it
- After it turns little brown add some chili powder and

coriander to it
- Add some salt to taste
- Fry onions in a separate pan. Then add fried onion, ginger paste and yogurt and cook it for about a minute
- Add some saffron (soaked in 3 tsp water) and garam masala for flavor
- Add a little bit of water if the gravy turns out to be too thick. Make sure that the spices are infused well with the chicken
- Cover the pan and allow it to cook for 15 minutes on low flame, stir it occasionally
- After 15 minutes your chicken korma is ready

Keema mutter

Keema mutter is a spicy and delicious recipe and is not a typical curry. This is a dry dish with boneless goat or chicken and can be eaten with naan or Tandoori roti

Ingredients:

- 1 lb goat meat (minced)
- ½ cup ghee
- 1 cup green peas
- 4 Cloves
- 2 tsp cumin seeds
- 4 Peppercorns
- 1 piece small cinnamon
- 2 Bay leaves
- 1 Black cardamom
- 1 tsp ginger paste
- 1 cup onions, grated
- 2 cups tomatoes chopped
- 1 tsp garlic paste
- 1 tbsp coriander powder
- Salt
- ½ tsp chili powder
- ½ tsp turmeric
- Cilantro leaves chopped

Preparation:

- First heat the ghee in a pan and then add the cumin seeds to it along with cinnamon, cloves, cardamom, peppercorn and bay leaves
- Add some garlic when the seeds start to splutter. Also add the onions and ginger and stir-fry till the fat separates
- Then add salt, tomatoes, turmeric, coriander powder and chili powder
- Continue to stir-fry, increase heat to high and add the minced goat meat and the peas.
- You need to stir it for some time till the meat gets fried completely. Then you need to lower the heat and cook it few more minutes. You will start seeing oil coming from the

meat.
- Now Keema mutter is ready to be served
- Garnish and serve it with chopped cilantro leaves

Spicy Fish Curry

This is a spicy Fish Curry which is a delicious and mouthwatering dish of North East India. It has its origin at the native state of Assam. This dish is mainly used with rice. You can use any white fish of your choice for this recipe.

Ingredients:

- 1-2 large white fish (like tilapia) cut in pieces
- 2-3 medium tomatoes
- 1 medium onion
- 3 green chilies
- hint of Turmeric powder
- cooking oil for frying
- Salt
- 1 tsp of Fenugreek seeds
- Fresh cilantro leaves

Preparation:

- First the fish needs to be marinated with turmeric powder and salt. Keep it marinated for 45 minutes.
- Take oil in a pan turn on medium heat. Add fish pieces and fry them . Make sure to fry from both sides properly. But do not over fry the fish. Take it out of the pan and keep aside.
- Add fenugreek to the oil and set the flame to medium. Wait till the spices splutter
- Add chopped onions to the oil and fry it till it turns light brown.
- Add the chopped tomatoes along with turmeric powder, green chilies and salt. Make sure to mix them properly.

- Cover the pan and let it cook till the tomatoes turn soft. After 10 minutes mash the tomatoes and add some water
- When the curry mixture starts to boil, add the fried fish and cook it on high flame for 12 minutes
- Add the chopped cilantro leaves and stir the mixture gently. After 3 minutes, remove the pan from your oven.

Your delicious Fish Curry is ready to be served, enjoy with white steamed rice.

Masala Zinga

Masala Zinga is a traditional Mughlai dish and is very popular in Northern India. It's a spicy item with lots of spices and mouthwatering flavor.

Ingredients:

- Oil ¼ cup
- Prawns ½ kg
- Ginger garlic paste 1 tbsp
- Onion chopped 2
- Chili powder 1½ tsp
- Coriander powder 1½ tsp
- Tomatoes chopped 2
- Green chilies chopped 6
- Cilantro leaves
- Turmeric ½ tsp
- Crushed red pepper ½ tsp
- Salt 1 tsp
- Dry fenugreek leaves 1 tsp
- few Curry leaves

Preparation:

- Heat ¼ cup of oil in a pan
- Next fry 2 chopped onions until they turn golden brown in color
- Add 1 table spoon of ginger garlic paste to it and also add 2 chopped tomatoes
- Add 2 table spoon of chili powder and 1 table spoon of turmeric powder along with 2 table spoon of turmeric powder

- Add salt to taste and 1 table spoon of crushed red pepper
- Fry all these spices properly until the oil floats at the top
- Then add ½ kg washed and cleaned prawns (shrimp) along with 4-6 chopped green chilies
- Add 2 table spoons of cilantro leaves along with 1 table spoon of fenugreek leaves.
- Simmer the entire mixture for a couple of minutes
- The dish is almost ready. Lastly, add slice of ginger along with curry leaves.

Your Masala Zinga is ready to be served with rice.

Goan Prawns Curry

Have you ever tried any Goanese cuisine? If you haven't, then Goan Prawn Curry would be the perfect dish to start with. Although this is not North Indian dish I am including it just because its just an amazing dish . This dish was introduced by the Portuguese who once established their colony in Goa

Ingredients:

- 500 Gram Prawns (Shrimp)
- 1 tsp Turmeric
- Salt
- 2 Cup Coconut milk
- 200 Gram Onions, chopped
- 2 Tbsp Oil
- 2 Green chilies
- 4-5 whole red chilies
- 1 tsp Coriander
- 1 tsp Cumin seeds
- 6 Black pepper
- ½ tsp Turmeric
- 1 Ginger
- 6 Cloves
- ¼ Cup Vinegar

Preparation:

- Start with grinding all the spices together properly with vinegar
- Get the prawns. Wash and dry them on paper towel.

Then you need to dust the prawns properly with salt and turmeric. Once it is prepared, keep it aside

- Take chopped onions and fry them in high flame. You need to fry the onion till they turn light brown
- Add the ground spices masala and then add the prawns to the mix.
- You need to fry this mixture for some time, till the prawns turn pink
- After the prawns have turned pink and are crispy, it is time to add coconut milk to the mixture.
- Cook it for another 5 minutes; Your dish is almost prepared.
- In the final step, you need to simmer it for 5 minutes garnish with green chilies

The delicious Goan Prawn Curry is now ready to be served with rice.

Achari Chicken

Achari Chicken or Achari Murg is another North Indian dish which was introduced by the Mughals. It is a spicy dish and contains wide varieties of Ingredients.

Ingredients:

- 2 lb Chicken
- 2 tbsp cooking oil
- 250 gm yogurt
- 3 tomatoes
- 4-5 onions
- 2 tbsp ginger-garlic paste
- 6-7 large Green chilies
- 1½ tsp fennel
- 1½ tsp Jeera
- 1½ tsp mustard
- Juice of one large Lemon
- Red chili Powder, Salt and Turmeric powder to your taste
- 1½ tsp Kalonji

Preparation:

- Take some oil and then heat it in a heavy saucepan.
- Add sliced onions and fry it till it turns into golden brown color
- Add sliced tomatoes and cook the mixture for 5 minutes, till tomatoes get mushy.
- In the next step, you need to add chicken, along with garlic-ginger paste, yogurt, red chili powder, salt to taste, turmeric powder.

- Cover the saucepan and cook on medium heat till chicken is half cooked
- Roast jeera, mustard, and kalonji together in a separate pan till the mixture turns into light brown. Grind the mixture to powder
- Add some turmeric to the mixture and then add some lemon juice to it. Grind the powder properly till it turns into a thick paste
- Add the paste to the chicken gravy and cook it for 10 minutes
- Add chilies to the chicken and cook at a low heat for 10-20 minutes on low flame.

Achari Chicken is now ready to be served

Saag Chicken

This is a dish with a wonderful blend of chicken and spinach. Great to get both your proteins and vegetables in one dish. It is not too spicy and can be taken with rice, roti and can also be used as an appetizer

Ingredients:

- 1 tbsp vegetable oil
- 4 boneless skinless chicken breasts
- ½ clove garlic, finely chopped
- ½ teaspoon dried oregano leaves
- salt
- ¼ tsp pepper
- 2 cup water
- medium plum tomatoes, sliced
- 6 oz baby spinach leaves
- ½ cup cream

Preparation:

- Heat oil in a large frying pan on low heat
- Add onion and cook for at least 3 minutes until onion becomes translucent.
- Add ginger and garlic to it and keep stirring for 2 minutes
- Add coriander, cumin, paprika, turmeric and salt
- Cook for a minute till the spices turn brown and then add them to the tomatoes
- Add cinnamon stick, cream and water to it
- Wash and squeeze the spinach properly so that any

excess liquid in it can be removed. Add spinach to the pan.

- Lower the heat and then cover the pan. Cook it for 5-8 minutes
- Add chicken and cook it for 20 minutes on medium flame till chicken is fully cooked.

The delicious Chicken in Spinach is now ready to be served

Chicken Jalfrezi

This is a very popular Mughlai dish, full of rich flavours. Its made using boneless chicken usually breast pieces and is best eaten with butter naan or Tandoori roti. Lets check the method.

Ingredients:

- 6 long green chilies
- 4 boneless skinless chicken breasts
- 2 tbsp sunflower or other cooking oil
- 2 garlic cloves
- 3 ripe tomatoes, chopped
- 1 tbsp ground cumin
- 1 tbsp garam masala
- 1 tsp turmeric powder
- salt
- 200ml cold water
- 2 tbsp yogurt
- 1 medium onion
- 1 green pepper chunks
- 2 tomatoes

Preparation:

- At first, heat oil in a pan and fry garlic and onion on medium heat for 5 minutes
- Add salt, turmeric and chili powder in a separate bowl and mix well

- Then add pieces of chicken breast to the mixture. Fry it for 15 minutes until it changes color
- Stir the ginger, garlic, tomatoes, coriander and cumin into the pan and then reduce the heat until the mixture is simmering.
- Cover the pan and cook it for half an hour. Don't forget to stir occasionally
- Add green pepper chunks. Cook it for 10 more minutes and you dish is ready to be served

Appetizers

Chapli Kabab

This is traditional Mughal dish which is soft and tender. If you are looking for something dry yet spicy protein to eat, then this one would just be the perfect choice for you

Ingredients:

- 2 lb Beef minced
- 1 tbsp White cumin
- 1 tsp Coriander leaves
- 4 pieces Green Chili chopped
- 3 pieces Tomato chopped
- 3 tsp Red chilies (crushed)
- 1½ tbsp Pomegranate seeds crushed
- 2 tsp Ginger pieces
- 1 tsp Black pepper
- ½ Onion chopped
- 1 Egg
- 6 tbsp Corn Flour
- Oil as needed
- salt as needed

Preparation:

- Take the minced beef in a pot. Add salt, coriander, diced tomato, green chili, crushed green coriander, red chilies, ginger, mint, pomegranate seeds, onion, black peeper, corn flour, and egg to the mix. Mix all the Ingredients properly like kneading flour.
- Once all the Ingredients are properly mixed, make small pieces of balls out of it
- Take oil in a large frying pan and heat it on high flame
- Fry the balls for 3 to 4 minutes until they turn reddish brown.
- Take the fried balls in a plate. Add some sliced onions

and the delicious chapali kabob dish is ready to be served

Mutton Chops in a curry

Looking for something spicy to eat as appetizer or entree? In that case Mutton chops would just be the perfect option for you. It's a mouth watering dish with delicious taste

Ingredients:

- 1 lb Goat Mutton chops
- 3 onions
- 2 tbsp of ginger and Garlic paste
- 4 Tomatoes
- 3 tsp of Red Chili powder
- 1½ tsp of coriander powder
- 2 tsp of chaat masala
- 2 tsp of Garam Masala powder
- Salt to taste
- Oil
- cooking soda

Preparation:

- Add oil in a pressure cooker, start on medium heat and then add garlic and ginger paste to it
- Add onion and tomato and then stir it for a while till they blend well each other
- Add mutton chops, salt and then fry for 3 minutes. Then add coriander, chili powder along with a pinch of cooking soda and hot water
- Close the pressure cooker and leave it for 15 minutes till the mutton is cooked
- After 15 minutes take it out of the oven and allow it to cool. This will automatically add some gravy to thicken

- Add some chat masala along with garam masala and then cook till the gravy turns almost dry
- Mutton chop is ready to be served; Sprinkle coriander leaves before serving it

Tandoori Chicken

Tandoori chicken is one of the most iconic Indian dishes and is known all over the world for its yummy and delicious flavor as well as its texture. It is cooked in a special oven called tandoor. But don't worry if you don't have tandoor oven at home, we will show you how to make it at home. We are showing the method using oven but you can replace it using outdoor barbecue. The key to good Tandoori chicken is marination of the chicken with spices.

Ingredients:
Chicken leg quarters – 6

For the marinade
- 3 tbsp ginger garlic paste
- 4 tsp red chili paste
- 2 tsp chaat masala
- 1 tbsp oil
- 3 tbsp curd
- ½ lemon juice
- salt

For Tandoori Masala (if you want to make your own)
- 2 Cinnamon sticks
- Black pepper
- Cardamom seeds
- Cloves
- Turmeric

You can skip this if you can get the tandoori masala directly from an Indian grocery store.

Preparation:

Marinade:
- Take a bowl and add ginger along with chili paste, chaat masala, curd, oil and lemon; then mix them properly
- Rub the marinade on chicken pieces properly
- Chicken should be marinated for an hour if possible

Tandoori Masala:
- In a flat pan, add all dry spices along with bay leaf and

turmeric powder.
- Once done, Grind these spices into fine powder; thats your tandoori masala

Procedure:
- Stuff the Tandoori masala on the marinated chicken leg pieces and keep aside for 10-15 minutes
- Start your home oven and set it to 400 deg Fahrenheit.
- On a roasting pan arrange the chicken pieces and roast in oven for 40 minutes, rotate in between and add spice mix paste often to keep the chicken moist. Care must be taken to keep chicken from becoming too dry.
  Serve the hot and delicious tandoori chicken with green salads

Seekh Kabob

This is another traditional North Indian dish usually done with lamb meat but can be done with chicken also. It is very popular in Punjab and Northern part of India and are usually used as appetizers

Ingredients:

- 1 Cup chicken dark Meat (minced)
- 1 tsp Ginger garlic paste
- 1 Egg
- ½ tsp Garam masala
- ½ tsp Cumin powder
- few Bread crumbs
- 1 medium Onion
- 1 tsp oil
- ½ tsp chili flakes

- ½ tsp Coriander powder
- 2 tsp Lemon juice
- Salt

Preparation:

- Grind the minced chicken, chili flakes, garlic and ginger paste, coriander powder, lemon juice, garam masala, cumin powder and salt in food processor and grind it finely.
- Make a paste of the onion. The add onion paste, egg yolk, bread crumbs, egg and oil. Grind the mixture together. Keep the mixture in fridge for an hour before starting next step.
- Grease the skewers so that the meat wont stick to it. Take a portion of the mixture in hand and spread it onto each skewer. Flatten the meat into a thin shape around each skewer.
- Grill the kebabs on barbecue grill or grill pan until meat is cooked well. Keep adding the paste in between to avoid the kabobs from getting dry.
- Once done touch up with lemon and garnish with fresh cilantro or mint chutney.

Vegetarian Dishes

Aloo Mutter Sabzi

Looking for some vegetarian North Indian dishes? In that case, Aloo Mutter kee Sabzi would just be the perfect option for you. It is delightful and can be eaten with almost anything like roti, paratha or rice.

Ingredients:

- 1 Cup or 200 gram Fresh Green Peas
- ¼ Cup Fresh Cilantro Leaves chopped
- 2 tbsp Ginger-Garlic Paste
- 3 medium Potatoes (chopped into cubes)
- Cooking Oil
- Salt
- 3 medium Tomatoes
- 2 medium Onions (finely chopped)
- 1 tsp Mustard Seeds
- 1 tsp Cumin Seeds
- ¼ tsp Asafoetida Powder
- 1 tsp Turmeric Powder
- 1 Dried Red Chili Powder
- 2 tsp Coriander Powder
- 1 tsp Garam Masala Powder
- ¼ tsp Dried Fenugreek leaves

Preparation:

- Heat the oil in a pan and then lightly fry the cubed potatoes for 5 minutes. After that, remove the potatoes from the pan and set aside.
- Put mustard seeds in the pan and wait for it to splutter
- Add cumin seeds along with Asafoetida powder and allow it to cook
- After 1 minute add chopped onions and saute it till onions turn brown
- Add turmeric powder and mix it properly. Then add ginger and garlic paste and cook on medium heat
- Add chopped tomatoes, coriander leaves and cook on

high heat for a minute
- Add green peas and let it cook for 10 minutes cover lid closed.

The dish is ready to be served , garnish with cilantro.

Green Bean Sabzi

This is another vegetarian dish which is used in India. It is light in taste and can be eaten with roti or parathas

Ingredients:

- 1½ cup chopped green beans
- ½ teaspoon cumin seeds
- salt
- ¼ teaspoon dry mango powder
- ½ teaspoon coriander powder
- ¼ teaspoon turmeric
- 1 medium chopped onion
- ½ teaspoon red chili powder
- 2 dried red chilis
- 1 medium finely chopped green chili
- 1-2 teaspoon oil
- ¼ cup water

Preparation:

- At first, heat a non-stick pan over moderate flame and add cumin seeds along with dried red chilies
- Wait till the cumin seeds turn into golden color and then add onions to it. Fry till the onions turn brown
- Add turmeric powder along with green chilies and dry mango powder. Also add coriander powder and red chili powder
- Stir the mixture for few seconds and then add the beans
- Add some water to the pot and cover it for 15 minutes

- After cooking it for 15 minutes, transfer to a serving bowl
- Add cilantro leaves and onion rings on top

It is now ready to be served

Baigan Bharta

Baigan Bharta is a very popular dish in North India. With mild spices, it tastes wonderful and the smell itself is mouth watering

Ingredients:

- 3 medium eggplants (roughly 1 pound)
- 2 tablespoons vegetable oil
- 1 teaspoon cumin seeds
- 2 medium onions (finely chopped)
- 1 tablespoon garlic paste
- 1-inch ginger grated
- 2 large tomatoes chopped
- ½ teaspoon coriander powder
- ½ teaspoon cumin powder
- ½ teaspoon garam masala
- cilantro
- Optional: 2 green chilies

Preparation:

- Take the eggplants and put them on medium flame. Keep them on the flame for 5 to 6 minutes until they get roasted
- Take the eggplants out of the flame once they turn black and brown and then slowly, start removing the skin. Once skin is removed, mash the eggplants
- Take oil in a pan and heat it for a couple of minutes
- Add finely chopped onions to the oil and then fry them, till they turn brown in color
- Add ginger-garlic paste and then add chopped tomatoes

- Add red chilies, coriander powder, garam masala, turmeric and salt. Stir them properly. Add the mashed eggplant and stir it properly
- Allow the mix to simmer for 10 minutes
- Add garam masala powder, mix well and your dish is ready to be served

Cholay Masala

Cholay, also known as Chana Masala is another very popular North Indian veg dish. Its usually served with a puri called bhature and people use this dish for breakfast as well as dinner.

Ingredients:

- 2 cup soaked chickpeas or 2 cans
- 4 sliced green chili
- 5 garlic cloves
- 2½ tablespoon coriander powder
- 1 teaspoon powdered red chili
- 4 tablespoon sunflower oil
- 2 chopped onion
- 3 cup chopped tomato
- 1 inch grated ginger
- 1 teaspoon turmeric powder
- 2½ tablespoon cumin powder
- 1 teaspoon garam masala powder
- salt

Preparation:

- Keep 2 cups of dry chickpeas soaked in lukewarm water overnight. Alternatively use one can of chickpeas, washed and drained.
- Heat oil on medium flame. Add chopped onions and fry them till they turn brown in color
- Once the onions turn brown add garlic and ginger to it and then reduce the flame. Cook for 3 to 4 minutes

- Now add tomatoes, turmeric powder, coriander powder, red chili and cumin powder. Cook till the oil gets separated
- Add the soaked chickpeas and pour in 3 cups of water
- Add coriander leaves and sprinkle salt to taste. Cook covered for 20 minutes on high heat
- Add garam masala and mix it well. Cover the pan and cook it for 3-5 minutes
- Once it gets cooked completely, transfer it to a bowl. Add sliced tomatoes and onions on top of it along with coriander leaves
  The dish is ready to be served with puri

Dal Tadka

Dal tadka is a dish which can be found anywhere in India. It has its origin in the state of Punjab however, is popular all over the country

Ingredients:

- 1 cup washed & drained moong dal
- 1 teaspoon ginger paste
- ½ teaspoon asafoetida
- 2 small diced onion
- ½ teaspoon mustard seeds
- 3 sliced & slit green chili
- ½ teaspoon cumin seeds
- salt as required
- 1 red chili
- 4 cloves chopped garlic
- 5 tablespoon vegetable oil
- 6 curry leaves
- 1 teaspoon turmeric
- 4 finely chopped tomato
- ½ teaspoon fenugreek seeds
- 1 teaspoon red chili powder

Preparation:

- Add washed moong dal in the pressure cooker. Add 4 cups water and heat it on medium flame. Cook the dal for half an hour until it turns mushy
- Then bring the flame down and make sure to stir in between
- Add cooking oil to a separate pan and add mustard seeds

along with red chili

- Add asafoetida, once the seeds start to splutter add ginger paste, red chili powder, garlic, curry leaves, cumin and chopped onions. Once the onion turns brown add chopped tomatoes and fry them along with the mixture for 6 minutes on low flame
- Add the mushy dal to the mixture and then add salt to it
- Simmer the dal on medium flame for 15 minutes and keep stirring it
- Switch the flame off once the dal is done and transfer the daal to a bowl
- Add cilantro leaves on top and sprinkle with chaat masala

Your dish is ready to be served

Masoor ki Daal

This is a very popular North Indian dish and is usually used with rice but can be enjoyed with Roti also. The steps of preparation are quite simple

Ingredients:

- 1 Cup Whole Masoor Dal (Indian Brown Lentils)
- 1 Medium Sized Onion
- 2 Large Tomatoes
- 3-4 Garlic Cloves
- 1 inch Piece of Ginger
- 1-2 Green Chilies
- 1 tsp Cumin Seeds
- 1/8 Teaspoon of Asafoetida (Heeng)
- 1½ Teaspoon Coriander Powder
- ½ Teaspoon Garam Masala
- ½ Teaspoon Turmeric Powder
- Salt
- 1 tsp Ghee
- ¼ Cup Coriander Leaves
- 1 Teaspoon Red Chili Powder

Preparation:

- Wash masoor dal in cold water. Then place it in a pressure cooker. Add 3 cups cold water along with turmeric powder and 1 tsp of salt; Mix it properly
- Pressure cook it for 15-20 minutes in the cooker
- Wait till the pressure cooker cools down and then open the lid
- Make sure that the dal is soft but not mushy

- Heat oil in a separate pan and add cumin seeds and allow them to splutter.
- Add Asafoetida into it; the add chopped onions along with ginger garlic paste and chili powder.
- Now add the cooked dal to the mix and cook till the mixture turns golden yellow for another 10 minutes.
- Add coriander leaves and chopped onions on top to garnish

The dish is ready to be served

Rice Dishes

Khichri

Not in a mood to cook full dinner course? Go for a plate of Khichri. It's easy to prepare and also tastes delicious.

Ingredients:

- ½ cup small grain Rice (Jasmine rice)
- ¼ cup Toor dal
- ¼ cup Moong Dal
- 2 tablespoons Ghee
- 1 teaspoon Cumin Seeds
- 6-8 whole Peppercorns
- 2 Bay leaves
- 4-5 Cloves
- 2 whole Cardamoms
- 1 teaspoon grated Ginger
- 1 Green Chili
- 6-8 Cauliflower Florets
- 1 Potato quartered
- 1 large Carrot, peeled and cut into 1 inch pieces
- 8-10 French Beans, cut into 1 inch pieces
- 1/2 cup frozen or fresh Green Peas
- 1 teaspoon Turmeric
- 1/2 teaspoon paprika Powder
- Salt

Preparation:

- Wash rice properly along with the toor dal and soak them in water for at least an hour.

- Take ghee and heat it in a pressure cooker and then add the peppercorn, cumin seeds, cloves, bay leaves, green chilies, ginger and cardamoms. Let the mixture cook on medium flame for 2 minutes
- Make sure to drain all the water out of the lentils and rice and then add them to the pressure cooker. Dry roast it for 5 minutes, till you get a nutty aroma. Make sure to not burn them
- Add all the vegetables, paprika powder, turmeric and salt along-with 3 cups cold water and pressure cook it for 15-20 minutes
- The dish is ready to be served with raita or chutney.

Jeera Rice

Looking to add some flavor to your rice dish? Jeera Rice would be the perfect option.

Ingredients:

- 1 cup long grain Basmati Rice
- 2 cups Water for soaking
- 1 tablespoon Ghee
- 1 Bayleaf
- 1 inch Cinnamon Stick
- 4-5 Cloves
- 1 teaspoon Cumin Seeds
- 1 Green Chili chopped
- 1/2 teaspoon Salt
- cilantro leaves

Preparation:

- Wash Basmati rice twice and then soak it in water for 30 minutes
- Then drain the water from the rice before cooking
- Heat ghee in a pot and add whole spices to it along with the cumin seeds
- Add chopped chilies once the cumin seeds start to splutter
- Add rice and cook on medium flame for 3 minutes
- Add salt and 2 cups of water to the rice and then mix it properly
- Bring the rice to a boil and then reduce the heat to simmer
- Cover it and cook it for 6-10 minutes

- Make sure not to overcook, you can stir in between, else you might end up burning it
- The dish is almost ready to be served
- Add some cilantro leaves on top along with some green chilies

The dish is ready to be served with dal or raita

Hyderabadi Chicken Dum Biryani

Chicken Biryani is one of the most popular of Indian dishes. Introduced by the Mughals in the Hyderabad region it is one of the most delicious dish made of rice and chicken. It takes some preparation and patience as the dish is slow cooked but the end result will just amaze you.

Ingredients:

- 2 lb. Chicken drumsticks or leg quarters
- 2 onions
- 10 gm clove
- 2 bay leaf
- lemon juice
- 2 tsp ginger garlic paste
- 1 pound basmati rice
- 200 gm clarified butter
- 1 cup yogurt
- 2 cinnamon stick
- 3 oz cream
- ½ teaspoon cumin seeds
- 3 cups whole wheat flour
- cardamom

Preparation:

- Take a large bowl and mix yogurt with red chili powder, turmeric powder, cumin powder, coriander powder, along with ginger and garlic paste.
- Mix all the ingredients alongwith salt and add pieces of chicken into the mixture. Put it in the fridge to marinate for few hours.
- Heat clarified butter or ghee in a deep bottomed pot. It

should have a tight fitting lid. Put the pot on medium flame and add bay leaf, cloves, cinnamon stick and cumin seeds. Wait for the spices to sputter

- Now add cut onion and marinated chicken into it.
- Add ginger and garlic paste to the chicken mix, and mix them well for a minute.
- In the next step add the beaten yogurt and sauté the chicken till the oil separates.
- When the oil is separated, add cardamom powder into it and sauté the chicken for a minute.
- Add water and cook the chicken on low-medium flame. Put the lid on the pot till the chicken is half cooked.
- Separately boil water in a pan and add salt and lemon juice. Once the water reaches boiling temperature add basmati rice and cook till the rice are half cooked, checking often.
- Open the copper pot lid of the chicken mixture and layer the rice on top of the cooked chicken. Above the rice layer, add ghee and cream. Garnish with cilantro or mint leaves, saffron and fried onions.
- Knead dough from the whole wheat flour and line the lid with it. Seal the copper pot and let it cook over medium flame for 20-30 minutes. Once the Biryani is cooked, slowly remove the dough and discard.

- Serve it hot with raita.

Mutton Biryani

This is another type of Biryani which is quite famous in India. The tender goat mutton well mixed with the rice makes it a delicious dish, cooking method is similar to chicken biryani. Just the time needed to cook the goat meat is little longer than chicken.

Ingredients:

- 2 pound goat mutton
- 2 green cardamom
- ½ cup ghee
- 1 bay leaf
- 1 tbsp turmeric
- few strands of saffron
- 2 tbsp ginger paste
- ½ cup cashew halves
- ½ cup raisins
- 1 teaspoon garam masala powder
- 1 cinnamon stick
- ½ cup fresh cream
- 3-4 whole red chili
- 2 teaspoon cumin seeds
- 2-3 tbsp garlic paste
- 2 cup basmati or long grain rice

Preparation:

- We will start by washing the mutton pieces thoroughly with water rinse completely. Next, add some salt, turmeric, garlic paste to it. Rubdown well so that the marination spreads evenly. Leave it in fridge for few hours.
- When you are ready to cook, Remove the mutton from the refrigerator and allow it to come down to room temperature. This step is important for the proper cooking of the meat.
- Meanwhile cook the basmati rice separately but make sure its only half cooked and keep aside to cool.
- Mix the strands of saffron in few tsp of water or milk. Heat clarified butter or ghee in pan and fry cashews and raisins, then aside for garnishing.

- Take onions, slice them and fry well. Keep half of the fried onions aside for garnishing.
- Heat ghee in a deep bottomed pot with fitting lid. Add bay leaf, cardamoms and cumin. Allow them to burst.
- Next add cinnamon sticks, whole red chilies and marinated mutton pieces. Add onions, ginger garlic paste, sliced onions and cook on high heat covered for 5 minutes. Check if the mutton is tender now.
- Now add the masalas and keep roasting the mutton till it starts spreading oil.
- Remove the mutton from the pan. In the same pan add a layer of cooked rice, followed by a layer of mutton and then again a layer of rice. Between each layer, sprinkle the cashew raisin mixture.
- Add rice on the top now. Separately add the saffron water and cream. Pour this evenly over the rice.
- Cover the lid and cook on low flame for 10-20 minutes. Once done garnish with onions, mint, cilantro and serve hot with raita.

Basmati Pulao

Basmati rice is a famous type of Indian rice and is used in preparing some of the best dishes. Basmati Pulao is one of them and used as staple food.

Ingredients:

- Basmati Rice 2 cups
- Carrots 1 medium
- Cinnamon 1 inch stick
- Cloves 2-3
- Bay leaf 1
- 1 medium onion chopped
- Cumin seeds 1 teaspoon
- 2-3 Carrots cut into strips
- Cauliflower florets 1/4 cup
- French beans cut into ½ inch pieces 10-12
- Green chilies slit 2
- Salt

Preparation:

- Heat oil in a non-stick pan and then add cloves, cinnamon, bay leaf, cumin seeds in it. Fry all these ingredients till the cumin seeds change their color
- Add onions and sauté till they turn light brown
- Add cauliflower florets, carrot strips, green chilies and beans
- Toss the mixture well and then add basmati Rice.
- Mix them properly and then add salt to taste and 4 cups of water

- Mix all these ingredients properly and then bring them to a boil
- Cover them and cook well on low flame till it gets cooked completely
- once ready, add cashews and fried peanuts on top

Basmati Pulao is ready to be served

Breads

Roti Paratha

Paratha is a kind of Indian bread, made of flour and other ingredients. It is a very popular food item in India and can be eaten with different types of curries.

Ingredients:

- 2 cups of wheat flour, which can be substituted with all purpose flour
- 2 tbsp cooking oil
- ¼ tbsp salt
- 2 tbsp ghee or oil
- Water

Preparation:

- Take a big bowl and mix flour, salt and oil.
- Keep on adding little water at a time in order to make light dough. You need to makes sure that the dough is not too sticky or too loose.
- Knead well in order to make sure that the dough is pliable and soft. Knead with moist figures . Wrap it in a moist cloth for half an hour
- Make small balls out of the dough.
- Use rolling pin and flatten them in long circular shaped balls. Use dry flour to avoid the dough from sticking to the

bottom of surface.
- Add little oil or ghee to a frying pan and wait till its hot
- Add the long circular parathas prepared onto the pan and roast them on the pan for 2 to 3 minutes from both sides
- The roti paratha is ready and can be served with pickles and any other kinds of curries

Keema Paratha

Keema Paratha is a North Indian dish. It is a wonderful blend of chopped mutton pieces with flour.

Ingredients:

- 250 gm minced goat mutton
- 3 teaspoon ghee
- ½ tablespoon cumin powder
- ½ teaspoon ginger
- ½ tablespoon garam masala powder
- ¼ tablespoon red chili powder
- 1 chopped green chili
- 1½ cup wheat flour
- Salt as required
- ½ tablespoon garlic
- ½ tablespoon coriander powder
- 2 chopped onion
- 1 tablespoon turmeric

Preparation:

- Wash and then add minced meat in a pan with oil, garlic and chopped ginger till they become tender.
- Add green chilies, cumin seeds, coriander and garam masala powder. Keep cooking well, this will be our filling material.
- In the mean time prepare the flour with salt, water and ghee and make small dough as we did for roti paratha.
- Add the mined meat to the center of the balls that you have prepared from the dough and then seal it properly
- Flatten the filled balls with fingers or both your palms and roll with rolling pins till they flatten long enough. The

paratha needs to be enough thick but not too thick.

- Add some ghee or oil in a pan and heat it on medium flame for 2 to 3 minutes
- After the oil has heated up, fry the flattened pieces of stuffed balls into it and fry for at least 4 minutes from both sides.
- The Keema paratha is ready to be served. It can be served with chutney

Aloo Paratha

Paratha is a very common food item in India. There are different types of Parathas available. Aloo Paratha is one of the most popular type and most north indians use it for breakfast alongwith curd and lassi. Very filling breakfast indeed.

Ingredients:

- 6-7 mashed, boiled, peeled potato
- 1-2 cup wheat flour
- 4 tbsp chopped coriander leaves
- 4 tablespoon melted butter
- Garam masala, Chaat masala and salt as per taste
- 4 finely chopped green chili
- ½ teaspoon black pepper
- 1 large onion
- 1 tablespoon red chili

Preparation:

- Boil the potatoes and once done, peel and mash them in a large bowl.
- Chop onions finely, also do same for green chilies and coriander leaves. Mix them to the potato mixture.
- Next add salt, and both masalas as needed, usually just a ½ tbsp each. The mixture should be mixed to a good consistency.
- Take wheat flour in a large bowl. Slowly add water to it and start kneading. Make it to a soft consistency
- Make medium balls of the dough and keep aside.
- Take one ball at a time, flatten it a bit and add small amount

of filling in the center. Close the sides by pulling the dough towards the middle. Now flatten them and start rolling with a rolling pin into round Parathas.

- Heat a griddle and roast the Parathas, once done on one side flip it to other side and add little bit of oil or clarified butter to it.
- The Parathas are ready to be served with hot curry or chutney

Poori

This is another popular Indian food item, made of wheat or all purpose flour. You can find Poori/Puri throughout the length and breadth of India. You can eat it with curry, dry sabzi and lots of other side dishes

Ingredients :

- 2 cup wheat flour
- ¾ tsp sugar
- salt to taste
- 1 tsp oil
- water as required, to knead
- oil for deep frying

Preparation:

- At first in a large mixing bowl, take wheat flour, sugar, and salt to taste. Add 1 tsp oil to the mix and combine all the ingredients well.
- Next add water and knead dough, ensure its not too soft.
- Divide the dough into smaller portions and roll to get to a long shape. Cut it further into small pieces with the help of knife.
- Make small balls the size of a pingpong ball and flatten. Grease the ball with oil on both sides. Roll the dough evenly into circular shapes using rolling pin. Puris should be thin but not too thin.
- Heat oil in a deep frying pan. When the oil is hot, drop rolled out puris.
- Press gently with the spoon to puff up. Once they puff, turn over. Fry the puri till golden brown all over.

The Puri is ready to be served

Soups

Chicken Soup

This dish requires no introduction. It is popular all over the world. Delicious and healthy at the same time, Chicken soup can be an excellent option to fill your bowl.

Ingredients:

- 1 pound chicken with bones
- 4 cups chicken broth
- 2 medium carrots
- 2 celery stalks
- 1 medium onion, chopped
- 1 bay leaf
- ½ cup wild rice
- 2 tablespoons chopped cilantro
- Salt

Preparation:

- Place the chicken pieces in a large pot. Add chicken borth and bring to a boil over medium heat.
- Now reduce the heat and let it simmer and cook for 20 minutes.
- Remove from heat, spoon out the chicken. Remove bones using fork and tongs. Meanwhile chop the carrot and celery in small pieces. Add these alongwith onion and bay leaf to the broth.
- Let it simmer and cook until the vegetables are cooked about 10-12 minutes.
- Stir in the wild rice, and cook until the rice is soft, 10 to 12

minutes. Also add the chicken meat kept aside in above step. Stir in the cilantro, and season with salt. Serve hot.

Tomato Soup

This is yet another very popular type of soup. It is delicious and nutritious at the same time. Looking for something quick and easy to full your bowl, then tomato soup would just be the perfect option for you

Ingredients:

- 4 cup ripe tomato
- 4 cloves
- 2 tablespoon butter
- 1 medium onion
- 2 cup veg stock

Preparation:

- Soak the tomatoes in lukewarm water with a pinch of salt. Next rinse it off with some cold water.
- In a stockpot combine chopped tomatoes, onion, cloves and 2 cups vegetable stock. Bring to a boil and simmer for about 20 minutes to blend all of the flavors.
- To add taste and aroma, you can add roasted garlic and cumins if needed. Remove from heat and run the mixture through a blender. Add sugar and salt as needed.
- Serve with croutons.

Chutneys

Poodina Chutney

Poodina or mint chutney is a kind of Indian sauce which can be used with all sorts of dishes. It is has a special flavor to it which makes it special. Besides, Poodina also had numerous health benefits to offer

Ingredients:

- ½ cup finely chopped mint leaves
- 1 cup finely chopped coriander leaves
- 2 garlic cloves
- 2 green chilies, chopped
- ¼ inch ginger piece
- sugar (optional)
- 1 teaspoon lemon juice
- salt to taste

Preparation:

- Take chili, garlic, sugar, ginger and salt in a food processor or grinder. Grind the ingredients properly
- Add mint leaves, coriander leaves, little water and one table spoon of lemon juice to it
- Grind all these ingredients again until the desired medium or smooth coarse consistency is achieved
- The Poodina chutney is ready to be served

Tip: It can be stored in a refrigerator and used over a period of 2 to 4 days

Raita

This is a side dish made of curd and other ingredients and is considered to be very useful for digestion. Besides, it also tastes delicious and can be used with numerous entree's.

Ingredients:

- 3 cups thick plain Yogurt
- 1 teaspoon Salt
- 1 teaspoon Cumin Powder
- 1 Green Chili, finely chopped
- ½ teaspoon Red Chili Powder
- 1 small Onion, finely chopped
- 2 Persian Cucumbers, finely chopped
- 1 large Tomato, finely chopped
- 1 Green Bell Pepper, finely chopped
- Cilantro for garnish

Preparation:

- Take the yogurt and add little water in order to dilute it properly.
- Usually Raitas are salty. Therefore, you have the liberty to add as much salt to it as long as it tastes good
- Then add all the ingredients to it and mix them properly
- Sprinkle some cumin powder and cilantro leaves on top of the dish.
  The raita is ready to be served

Green Coriander Chutney

Chutney is one of the most popular dishes in India. There are different types of Chutneys available in this part of the world. Coriander chutney is one of them. It's delicious and can be eaten with all kinds of fries

Ingredients:

- ½ cup chopped coriander leaves
- 2 tablespoons mint leaves
- 1 tablespoon groundnuts
- 1 green chili, chopped
- ½ inch ginger piece
- salt
- 1 tablespoon lemon juice

Preparation:

- Take ground nut, ginger, green chili, salt and sugar (optional) in a mixer grinder; Grind them properly until it becomes smooth
- Add mint leaves, coriander leaves, lemon juice along with water and then grind them again till the mixture turns into a thick paste
- The green coriander chutney is ready to be served
- Sprinkle some chaat masala om top before serving

Deserts

Mango Lassi

Lassi is a popular drink in India. It has its roots in the state of Punjab. This drink is made of curd with other ingredients added to it. Lassi tastes delicious and at the same time helps to quench thirst during the summers in India. You can add different fruits for different flavors. This one is using mango.

Ingredients:

- 1 cup plain yogurt
- ½ cup whole milk
- 1 cup mango puree or pulp
- sugar
- cardamom powder if desired

Preparation:

- Take all ingredients in a blender and blend it for about 2 minutes
- You can add some ice cubes to it while it is blending
- After the blending is done, pour it in a container. The mango lassi is ready to be served
- Sprinkle a little bit of cardamom powder on top and serve it
- Drinking it fresh is recommended but you can keep in the fridge for upto a day

Masala Chai

Chai or tea is a one of the most popular drinks in India. India is one of the largest producers of tea in the world and no wonder that here you will find verities of different types of teas. Masala chai is one of them

Ingredients :

- 1.5 cup of Water
- 1 cup of Milk
- 1.5 tsp of loose Black tea
- 1 tsp of Ginger (grated)
- 2-3 Tulsi leaves (optional)

Preparation:

- Take a small pot and boil the milk and water together
- Then add loose black tea and freshly grated ginger to it
- Boil on medium heat for nearly 2 minutes and then add tulsi leaves to it. Make sure to stir it properly
- Continue to boil in low heat for nearly 3 minutes, till the color starts to change and the consistency becomes little less watery
- After 3 minutes, the masala chai is ready. Use a strainer and pour it in a cup.

Gajar ka Halwa

In India there are lots of different types of sweets available. One of the most common one is Gajar ka Halwa. Made of carrot and other different ingredients, this dish is one of the most popular sweet items in India

Ingredients:

- 2 pound carrots
- 1½ litre milk
- few cardamoms
- few tbsp ghee
- ¼ cup sugar
- Almonds, raisins and dates (optional)

Preparation:

- Wash the carrots properly and then peel and grate them finely.
- In the next step, simmer the carrots in milk along with cardamom till the mixture is devoid of any water and the mix feels like a thick paste
- Then take ghee in a pan and heat it on low flame. Add the carrot mixture to it. Cook the mixture for 15 minutes at a medium flame
- Next add sugar and continue cooking till the mixture turns brownish red. The Halwa is almost ready to be served
- Add some dried fruits on top of the preparation and then serve it.

Gulab Jamun

Gulab Jamun is another popular sweet dish in India. Though it has its root in Northern India; however, it is very popular throughout the country.

Ingredients:

- 100 Gram Khoya (firmly packed)
- 1 tbsp all purpose flour
- ¼ tsp baking soda
- 2 cups Sugar
- 2 cups Water
- 2 tbsp Milk
- 1 tbsp cardamom powder
- Ghee

Preparation:

- Use the base of a flat metal bowl or the heel of your palm to mash the khoya and smoothen it out.
- In the next step, mix the baking soda and all purpose flour and then make firm dough out of it. It can be done with the help of a food processor
- Make sure that the dough is firm enough; however, pliable at the same time and it shouldn't feel dry. If it does, wet your palms and start working with the dough again
- Knead the dough in small size balls like pingpong balls, which are known as "jamuns". Make sure that they are smooth and without any cracks. As far as the shape is concerned, it can be either oblong or round
- Heat the ghee and drop the jamun balls in it. Fry them on

low heat till they turn golden in color. Once done drain the Jamuns out of the ghee and keep aside.

- Next take 2 cups of sugar and mix in lukewarm water in a pot; keep the pot on low heat. Keep heating till the syrup turns semi-thick. Stir till the syrup feels like a sticky syrup and not watery. The syrup is prepared.
- Now all you need to do is to dip the Jamuns in the syrup for a couple of minutes

The Gulab jamun is ready to be served

Final word

We hope this book would help you to cook delicious Indian dishes at home. Start today and start cooking!

Please rate us on amazon!

   If you have any suggestions or would like to subscribe to our mailing list for promotions on our upcoming books, please send an email to *royalbookpublishers@gmail.com*

Made in United States
Troutdale, OR
07/17/2023

11330661R00064